More Than Enough

Finding Comfort and Hope Through Jesus Christ in the Last Days

Theresa L. Bracey

© **Copyright 2021 - All rights reserved.**

The content contained within this book may not be reproduced, duplicated or transmitted without direct written permission from the author or the publisher.

Under no circumstances will any blame or legal responsibility be held against the publisher, or author, for any damages, reparation, or monetary loss due to the information contained within this book, either directly or indirectly.

Legal Notice:

This book is copyright protected. It is only for personal use. You cannot amend, distribute, sell, use, quote or paraphrase any part, or the content within this book, without the consent of the author or publisher.

Disclaimer Notice:

Please note the information contained within this document is for educational and entertainment purposes only. All effort has been executed to present accurate, up to date, reliable, complete information. No warranties of any kind are declared or implied. Readers acknowledge that the author is not engaged in the rendering of legal, financial, medical or professional advice. The content within this book has been derived from various sources. Please consult a licensed professional before attempting any techniques outlined in this book.

By reading this document, the reader agrees that under no circumstances is the author responsible for any losses, direct or indirect, that are incurred as a result of the use of the information contained within this document, including, but not limited to, errors, omissions, or inaccuracies.

Dedication

This book is dedicated to my loving parents, Taylor and Carolyn Bracey, who first introduced me to Jesus at a young age. They were wonderful parents who loved the Lord and instilled in me a love for Him. It is because of them that I am the woman I am today. They gave me the best gift any parent could give a child: Jesus. I am forever grateful for their love, support, and guidance. During the writing of this book, my beloved father sadly transitioned from labor to reward and is now in the arms of Jesus, along with my mother. May their souls rest in peace until we meet again.

Table of Contents

INTRODUCTION 1

CHAPTER 1: TROUBLE IN THE LAND 9

    IT'S NOT TIME TO FEAR AND PANIC 11

CHAPTER 2: PEACE IN THE MIDST OF CHAOS 17

    THE FAITH OF THOSE WHO HAVE GONE BEFORE US 19

CHAPTER 3: ON YOUR MARK, GET SET, GO! 25

    WHEN YOU FACE ADVERSITY, USE VIOLENT FAITH 31

CHAPTER 4: BELIEVE IT AND RECEIVE IT 45

    WALK IN GOD'S WAYS 48

CHAPTER 5: NO MORE SITTING AND LOOKING 59

    BE A VESSEL FOR GOD'S USE 63

CHAPTER 6: LIVING THE ABUNDANT LIFE 67

CONCLUSION 71

REFERENCES 79

Introduction

I grew up in a Christian family with so much love and guidance, especially from my mother. My mother loved the Lord and had a close personal relationship with Jesus. She was saved and had God's Holy Spirit within her. She was a woman of great faith and love for the Lord, and it showed in the way she treated and loved people. She was a role model of Christ's love to her loved ones and anyone else who had the privilege of crossing her path. Mom shone with God's love in everything she did.

I lost my mother to metastatic breast cancer when she was only 45 years old. I knew I had to reach deep within myself for the strength to go on, but I couldn't seem to find it, no matter how hard I tried. I had such an empty void inside that seemed to rip at my very being. I wondered how God could take my mother from me at such an early stage; my life had only just begun. She hadn't lived long enough, only for a short time. My mother wouldn't get the chance to see me get married or hold her grandchildren.

I constantly wondered how a loving God could take my mother from me when I was only 20 years old. We still had so much to do together, so many years to share in each other's lives. I still needed my mom to answer my questions about men and relationships, to go shopping with, and support me in my emotional journey through heartbreaks and unsure moments. I often thought, *Who is going to help me when I have a baby?* I wouldn't know what to do when I was pregnant or how I would emotionally handle birth or caring for a newborn.

I felt like a part of me had died. How could I go on without Mommy? I missed my mother so much, and I just wanted to see her again, be with her, touch her, and smell her sweet perfume one more time. My heart ached for her, and I knew I needed God to help me get through it. I longed to have her hug me in only the way she knew how, with so much love and affection. I could feel her love for me in the way she hugged and looked at me. I was broken, and I didn't know how to become unbroken.

You see, she was my best friend, and I loved her very much. It seemed like the world couldn't go on without my beautiful mother in it. But life seemed to go on as usual for everyone else around me, those who knew her, and those who didn't have the privilege of knowing her. People still got up each morning and went about their daily routines as if nothing had happened.

The news reports on TV, the buses, the taxis, and all other forms of transportation went on around me. I saw people on television laughing and being happy. Life had stopped for me; it was as though I was frozen in time, and my shattered pieces were falling all around me. I was inconsolably devastated, with no hope in sight, only my broken thoughts and an aching heart to keep me company.

I was angry with God. I thought, *How could God allow my mother to die when I still needed her so much?* I had prayed and asked God to heal her, but she still died. Yes, I was very angry with God, and I didn't want to live on this earth without my mother. I felt betrayed and all alone. I thought, *It's not fair. I can't go on unless Mommy is here with me.*

I thought of ways to take my own life. I cried and wondered why God would allow this travesty to happen. What had I done to deserve such pain and loss in my life?

I was always raised to believe that taking your own life was a sin, and people who did such an awful thing would never go to Heaven, but would spend eternity in hell. At that point, though, I didn't care about my life anymore. I felt I had nothing or no one to live for. I believed in God and did not want to go to hell for taking my own life, but what if I were in an accident and died that way? If I died in a car crash, it would be God's will, and that would be OK with me. I thought that maybe if I died in a car accident, I wouldn't go to hell. I was so desperate; all I wanted was to be with my mother.

I went out one night for a drive alone. I just needed some time and space to think. I had no plan or destination; I just needed to get away from it all. I set out driving around Monticello, then to the outskirts of the tiny village adjacent to it. I found myself in a town called Mountain Dale and was completely lost, but I didn't care. I began driving faster and turned recklessly around the curved roads. At one point, I drove on top of a mountain on a narrow road, with a cliff face below me. It was dark, there were no street lights to light the way, and the roads were difficult to see.

I kept driving faster and faster around those mountainous curves, hoping for the accident that would reunite me with my mother. I knew I would never see her again if I killed myself and landed in hell. I had no doubt my mother's soul was in Heaven with the Lord. It was indescribable to go through the hurt and pain of losing her at such a young age. I didn't know how I would be able to go on without her. I had no hope, and I just wanted the pain to stop and to be reunited with her again. If I could just get to her, I knew she could make it all right again.

Dealing with the loss of my mother was the first time in my life that I experienced real hurt and pain and such awful loneliness. I was not only lost in where my vehicle was taking me but lost inside of myself as well. I needed Jesus to take my steering wheel and direct me home then take control of my life. I didn't have an accident that night, and I somehow made it home safely.

When I think back to that night, I don't even know how I got home. I can only think it was God's infinite power and grace that steered me home. I was so lost, and I now know that the Lord was with me the whole time, guiding me and keeping me safe. Jesus was with me, giving me strength and holding me the whole time. He was right there with me; He never left my side, only I didn't know it at the time.

He loved and cared for me when I didn't care about myself. When I didn't care if I lived or died, the Lord Jesus Christ cared for me and protected me from danger. His mercy and His grace would not allow the enemy of this world, Satan, to kill me in a car accident. We need to remember that Satan can't destroy the true Gospel, so he does all he can to attack those who believe it. He tempts, divides, accuses, schemes, deceives, lies, stirs gossip, and provokes distrust. He feeds bitterness into our hearts, and the brain is his battlefield. If he is not feeding your brain with destructive thoughts, he is feeding someone else's so they will provoke your mind once again.

While traveling on life's journey, I have found that I cannot make it without Jesus. I have had many heartaches, disappointments, and moments of sadness and pain in my life, and through everything, Jesus carried me. God is good, and He loves me more than I love myself. God knows me better than I know myself.

> "Before I formed you in the belly I knew you . . ."
> (Jeremiah 1:5 King James Version)

> "According to how He has chosen us in Him before the foundation of the world, that we should be Holy and without blame before Him in Love" (Ephesians 1:4)

I would not be here today if it had not been for the Lord, who was on my side. He reached down and rescued me and saved me from dying in a car crash. In my darkest hour of great sadness and while mourning the loss of my mother, God was with me and He never left.

I later realized that I was wrong for being angry with God about the passing of my mother. I also realized I was being selfish for wanting her here just for myself. My mother was a beautiful gift from God, and she belonged to Him, as we all do. The Lord giveth, and the Lord taketh away. It is not for me to say when God can call anyone home if He chooses to do so. I am so thankful and blessed for the 20 years of my life that I was able to spend with my beautiful mother and for all the amazing memories God allowed me to have with her.

God is in control, and with all His infinite wisdom, He knows what's best. After the passing of my mother, I developed a stronger, closer relationship with the Lord, and it has only gotten better over the years. God has shown himself to be strong and mighty in my life. My life changed after the passing of my mother. I learned to depend on Jesus, and I knew my mother would want me to do just that. I can still hear her say, "Always put God first."

I wanted to make her proud of me, even though she was no longer with me. I wanted to be just like her: a strong, virtuous woman of God. I took comfort in knowing that I still had my dad, who was my rock when I needed a shoulder to cry on or someone to talk to about any and everything. I thanked God that I still had my dad. My dad and I were always close, but we became even closer after the passing of my mother. I didn't have my mother anymore, but I felt so blessed to still have my dad and my Heavenly Father.

I have come to realize that Jesus is more than enough for me. He is more than my mother, more than my father, more than a best friend, more than true love, more than anything good that I can think of. Jesus is more than enough. "For His anger endures but a moment; in His favor is life: weeping may endure for a night, but joy comes in the morning" (Psalm 30:5). My Lord and Savior Jesus Christ turned my weeping and mourning into gladness and unspeakable joy!

Chapter 1:

Trouble in the Land

> "It is not God's will that any should perish but that all should come unto repentance" (2 Peter 3:9)

> "The time is now to seek the Lord Jesus Christ while He may be found, call upon Him while He is near. Let the wicked forsake his way, and the unrighteous man his thoughts: and let him return unto the Lord, and He will have mercy upon him and to our God for He will abundantly pardon" (Isaiah 55:6–7)

> "Then Peter opened his mouth, and said, Of the truth I perceive that God is no respecter of persons" (Acts 10:34)

What He did for me, He will also do for you. He is the same God of today, yesterday, and to the end of time. Everything going on in the world today clearly shows us that we must repent from all sins and unrighteousness while we still have time to do so. There is so much evil, death, and disease in this world. "That we should also know that in the last days perilous times shall come" (2 Timothy 3:1). We are living in the last days, and Jesus is the soon-coming king.

The world is in desperate need of a savior, and that savior is Jesus Christ: the true and living Son of God, the King of Kings, and Lord of Lords. In this world of so much uncertainty, sickness, disease, sin-sick souls, and multitudes of people with no hope, there is hope in the name of Jesus. Now, with this new and deadly plague on the earth called coronavirus or COVID-19, the world needs Jesus like never before.

During this global pandemic and with so many people who have already lost their lives to COVID-19, we who are still alive on the earth have a chance to repent. That help is in Jesus Christ. He is our help in times of trouble and times of need. "I will lift up my eyes unto the hills, from whence cometh my help. My help cometh from the Lord, which made heaven and earth" (Psalm 121:1–2). Surely, with all these things going on, it is clear to see we are living in the last days. God warned us; He told us in His word that in the last days, perilous times would come.

Now is the time to seek Jesus while He may be found. Satan will always tell you, "Don't worry about it now; you can do it tomorrow." There may not be a tomorrow for you. Go do it now! Now is the time to pray and repent from all sins, mistakes, and wrongdoings that have happened in your life. Now is the time to love the Lord Jesus Christ our God with all your heart and with all your soul and with all your mind. This is the first and greatest commandment (see Matthew 22:37–38).

God promised to never leave us or forsake us, so we can trust that He will always be with us and take care of us. In Jesus Christ alone, all our hope is found. We do not have to fear what the future holds because we know who holds the future. God is bigger than any plague, disease, or enemy of this world. God is even bigger than COVID-19, and He is able to deliver us from this deadly plague that is killing millions of people on the earth.

It's Not Time to Fear and Panic

We have a massive challenge in life we must overcome. It is a constant battle; just when we think we have mastered it, we begin to recognize the symptoms once more. It then becomes time to place our focus on God again. Fear is not a mental state or a bad attitude. It is an evil spirit, and it does not come from God. "God did not give us a spirit of fear, but of power, and of love, and of a sound mind" (2 Timothy 1:7).

Fear is our most deadly opponent, and it is sent to torment our soul and destroy our human spirit. Fear can only affect us if we believe it and allow those thoughts to take hold of us. Fear will be the ultimate spirit that will be the demise of all mankind. Christians will move away from Jesus because of fear. Take control and remove it out of your life and replace that void with faith.

When we live in God's perfect love for us, He protects us. "There is no fear in love; but perfect love casts out fear: because fear has torment. He who fears is not made perfect in love" (1 John 4:18). God has a perfect love for us, and if we have a perfect love for Him, which we surely can have, then we know He is going to sustain us, so there is nothing to fear.

Don't be afraid of Satan; only be aware that he is prowling around and trying to trap and deceive you through your open gates. These open gates are your eyes, ears, nose, and sexual parts. Satan has been defeated and is at the footstool of God as he waits on punishment. If you are wondering why I use the Old Testament as well as the New Testament, God says in the book of Acts that all of

God's words have been engraved on the flesh tables of our hearts. You have been given authority over Satan. If you resist the devil, he will flee. Take your inspiration from the Holy Spirit.

We don't have to be afraid. If God did not give us the spirit of fear, then we know it's a spirit from the enemy of this world. Fear is the direct opposite of faith. When we fear, we are saying God is not enough. I want to tell you He is and He has this whole world in His hands. If you have faith, He will heal and help you.

It is not God's will that His children live in fear. We have to trust in God and His plan for our lives and know that through all the chaos that is going on in this world, God is still in control of it all. Now is not the time to panic, worry, or fear. Trust in the Lord, your God. Jesus knows the end from the beginning (see Isaiah 46:10).

Satan will constantly place fearful thoughts in your mind and use situations to create panic. To fear is a sin, and through this sin, you open a door for Satan to attack you. In fact, he wants you to believe you have COVID-19 or any other disease so he can give it to you. Disease and illness don't come from our God; it comes from Satan alone.

"Surely He has borne our griefs, and carried our sorrows: yet we did esteem Him stricken, smitten of God, and afflicted. But He was wounded for our transgressions, He was bruised for our iniquities; the chastisement of our peace was upon Him, and with His stripes, we are healed" (Isaiah 53:4–5). In other words, Israel assumed that Jesus was "smitten of God" and cursed by Him. And in fact, He was. He suffered on our behalf. He was our substitute, which means that the blow that should have come to us instead went to Him.

Jesus had no sin; He took our sins onto Him. Jesus is God in the flesh, and His life is worth more than the lives that will ever be born to this planet. So He paid the price on our behalf. He was afflicted and died on our behalf so we would not go to hell for our transgressions. He was bruised for our iniquities, meaning what He suffered was not at all for Himself, but for us. "The chastisement of our peace was upon Him" means that if peace between God and man was to be restored, all which Adam lost to Satan, then Jesus would have to bring it about through His death. This is a simple doctrine of the Gospel: Christ died for those of us who believe and give our lives to Him.

All other founders of religion base their claims upon their life teachings. When they died, their death was a calamity and without significance. Jesus' death was and is His Glory, a gift. It forms the imperishable foundation of the one and only salvation. His purpose in coming to Earth was to die. "And with His stripes, we are healed" definitely pertains to physical healing but is far greater in meaning than that. Its greater meaning refers to being healed of the terrible malady of sin.

"Malady" means the curse of sin. Jesus received 39 Roman whippings, and each whip held six tails. Each of those tails held a sharp cutting object, like glass or a sharp stone or hook. Consequently, there are 39 mainstream diseases in today's world, and the whippings are symbolic of these diseases. COVID-19 is just one of the diseases Jesus took onto His body. If we believe in faith, healing will come. If it's not our time to go home and be with Him, then Jesus will heal us.

Sickness and sin can be compared to each other. Let me explain. At first, sickness can be caught through carelessness, not eating the correct foods, or not looking after your body correctly. It can also be stress-related. People can catch colds from wearing fewer clothes than they should. Adam grew careless and did not pay attention to what Eve was up to in the garden. He then joined her in her sin. Adam removed the clothes or garments of his innocence, and he then became ill.

He wasn't allowed in the garden any longer and became bedridden. His sin turned the world from a paradise into a hospital. Sickness can come from an abundance of offspring, and according to Genesis 3:6, it can come through a generational curse because the covering of God was removed by mankind. The modern world explains it as genetics. Today, we have added to this problem by perpetrating other sins in our lives; therefore, we have made matters worse (see 2 Timothy 3:13).

God will take care of His people during this pandemic and at all times because He loves us. Now is the time for repentance, to humble ourselves and pray and seek God and turn from our wicked ways. Only then will God hear from Heaven, forgive our sins, and heal our land (see 2 Chronicles 7:14). I know God can do just what He said in His word. God loves us, and He is not willing that any should perish, but that all should come to repentance (see 2 Peter 3:9).

"For God so loved the world, that He gave his Only Begotten Son, that whosoever believes in Him should not perish, but have Everlasting Life" (John 3:16). We can come to Jesus just as we are. There is nothing we have to do to get ready; we can just come. Jesus will meet us wherever we are and in whatever state we are in. We can trust that He will save us and help us in our most difficult and darkest days.

He will accept us just as we are. His yoke is easy, and his burden is light. Jesus said, "Come unto Me, all you who labor and are heavy laden, and I will give you rest" (Matthew 11:28). "There is no respect of persons with God" (Romans 2:11). What He does for one, He will most definitely do for another.

It was Jesus who was there with me during the darkest days of my life. When I didn't want to go on, when I wanted to throw in the towel and give up on life, Jesus rescued me from myself, and He held onto me closely and wouldn't let me go. That's love, pure unconditional, agape love. I love the Lord Jesus Christ because He first loved me. Jesus died for my sins, rose from the dead on the third day, and is sitting at the right hand of the Father, interceding for His children. If Jesus saved me and rescued me, surely He will do it for you too.

This is a season that the Lord has made to allow all His children to come to Him. Seek Him now while He may be found during this global pandemic. He did not bring this pandemic, but He will bring it to good in our lives if we let Him. We are all in this together; no one should feel like they are alone. God the Father, Jesus the Son, and the Holy Spirit are with us in the Trinity as one God. We can make it with Jesus because He is enough.

Chapter 2:

Peace in the Midst of Chaos

With so many people afraid and uncertain about the state of the world during the coronavirus pandemic, we can be sure of one thing: Jesus is with us. The Lord said He would never leave us or forsake us in Hebrews 13:5. God's word is true. He "is not a man, that He should lie" (Numbers 23:19). Jesus loves us all; He loves the entire world, and He died for the sins of the entire world. I know Jesus loves me and saved me from my sins. Jesus rescued us from a life of sin and shame.

I chose to surrender my life to the Lord Jesus Christ and repent of all my sins, mistakes, wrong thinking, and wrongdoings. I then chose to be baptized in Jesus' name, and I received the gift of the Holy Ghost. This is a choice we all have; God does not force Himself on any of His children. He wants us to come to Him freely, of our own will. Jesus wants to have a relationship with His children and give us the desires of our heart. If we seek and trust Him and ask Him, God is faithful to do it (see Matthew 7:7).

Romans 8:5–10 explains that if we are flesh and of this world, we are in a phase of death. We do not belong to Him and have to change our spirit to a contrasting Spirit of God. We are reborn as a new creation in Him. The Holy Spirit makes us what we ought to be, which means we cannot do it ourselves. He performs all that He does within the confines of the Finished Work of Christ.

If you find yourself hungry for truth, you are being invited by the Holy Spirit to receive a greater revelation (see Proverbs 27:7–14). This is when the Holy Spirit will split the veil of flesh that keeps us from knowing the real truth. We can then get to know God intimately and witness the wonderful things from His law (see Psalm 119:18–19). As we become unveiled through truth, His hidden truths are revealed to us. This will attract others who may find us peculiar at first (see Exodus 19:5 and Deuteronomy 14:2). The word *peculiar* used in this context is a good thing, meaning out of the ordinary or rare.

Without further information and knowledge-containing scriptures, we cannot have a full revelation of Christ within us, even if we are born-again Christians. The Holy Spirit inscribes the words on our heart tablets, and this will have no value if we do not allow it to move in our lives (see Matthew 4:4 and James 1:21).

I am a witness to God's faithfulness. The Lord stayed with me through all my heartaches, disappointments, and times of trouble in my life. Jesus was right there with me too. When others left me and turned their backs on me, their rejection hurt, but Jesus never did; He was always with me, through every milestone and every situation. I can honestly say that Jesus is my very best friend. I thank and praise God for Jesus.

The Faith of Those Who Have Gone Before Us

Do you remember the story of the fiery furnace in the book of Daniel, chapter three? King Nebuchadnezzar ordered a gold statue to be set up near Babylon. This statue stood 27 meters high, and the sun shone over it. He made the statue into his god that he worshipped. He called men from far and wide, who traveled to see this idol dedicated in Babylon. A splendid ceremony was set up, and everyone arrived in their best attire or finest robes. The royal herald announced, "Listen to the king's command. In a moment, you will hear the trumpets, oboes, zithers, and harps playing. As soon as you hear the music sound, you must bow down and worship this golden statue. Anyone who doesn't obey will be hurled into the blazing furnace."

A signal was given, and the music sounded out. Everyone bowed down to worship except for Daniel's three friends: Shadrach, Meshach, and Abednego. Many people were jealous of the fame these three men had, who resided in Babylon at the time. They went directly to the king with the news that these men were not worshipping and didn't bow to the idol.

King Nebuchadnezzar was angry and sent for the three men. He told the men that the next time they disobeyed his command, he would throw them directly into the furnace. The three men replied and said they were not going to change their minds. Their God Elohim (God the Father) would protect them, and even if he didn't save them, they would still not worship any other God. The king was furious and shouted that the furnace should be made seven times hotter than before.

The soldiers tied up the men properly with very strong ropes and led them away to the furnace. As the soldiers approached the fire, the heat became unbearable, and when the furnace was opened, the soldiers managed to push the three men inside but died from the fumes and severe heat of the flames. Since the king had told the guards to report back to him and there was no sign of them returning, the king himself went to investigate the furnace area.

There, he discovered the dead guards on the floor near the furnace, and to his great amazement, he saw four men walking around in the furnace. The king called for them to come out of the furnace, but only Shadrach, Meshach, and Abednego came out. The king now knew that their God was with them always, even through the hottest fires. These three men had no sign of damage on them; they didn't even smell of smoke.

The king proclaimed that the God Shadrach, Meshach, and Abednego were worshipping was by far the greatest God of all. "Praise the king of the Jews!" he shouted. "He rescued His men because they trusted in Him. I will punish anyone who tries to mock their God." Everyone had to obey the king, and these three men became the most important and powerful men in the kingdom.

Then, in Daniel chapter 6, a different king, but an enemy, tried a similar approach. Daniel's work became outstanding, and men became jealous, plotting ways to get rid of him. The evil men approached King Darius and said that everyone had agreed that for 30 days, no one was allowed to worship any other god but the king. King Darius was flattered and signed and sealed the Medes and Persian. This meant that no one could change the decree, and punishment would stand.

Daniel realized he was being trapped, but his love for his God meant more than death. Daniel always prayed three times a day, and he opened the window as usual and knelt in front of it. He lifted his voice and worshipped God as always. His enemies kept a close watch and waited for Daniel, and they quickly ran to King Darius and reminded him that the law could not be altered for any reason. The king liked Daniel and was distressed that his trusted servant would be put to death. He tried all day to change the law and looked for many different methods, but he couldn't find a way out for Daniel.

The soldiers arrested Daniel and threw him into a large pit with starving lions. The king tossed and turned the whole night, and in the morning, he commanded that the rock be pushed aside. King Darius shouted to Daniel, "Daniel, has your God saved you from the lions?" Daniel answered, "Yes, your majesty! God has saved me by keeping the jaws of the lions shut." King Darius was thrilled and threw down a rope for Daniel.

The king was so furious that he had been deceived that he flung down the evil men and all their families to be eaten by the lions. The king sent out a message that everyone will respect Daniel's God, who rules forever. His kingdom will never end, and His power will last forever. He protects and rescues His people. He saved Daniel, and He will save you. God is the same God who saved the Israelites from Egypt when he opened up the Red Sea and opened the jail doors for Peter. He is the alpha and omega, the Mighty One, the overflowing, overloving, omnipotent, omnipresent Godhead in all its fullness.

His arm is never too short to help, and He never sleeps. He is always willing to answer your call and is always ready to rescue you from the miry pit. I don't know what I would do without Him in my life. Surely, I would be dead, lost forever in sin, and on my way to hell had it not been for the Lord, who was ever by my side. Jesus saved me. He never stopped loving me and interceding for me. Every time the enemy of this world tried to kill me, God's grace and mercy said, "No!"

Through every car accident I survived, I thanked God for His extended mercy and grace that saved my life and soul. "Jesus said unto Him, I am the Way, the Truth, and the Life: no man comes unto the Father, but by Me" (John 14:6). If you come through any other means, God the Father will not recognize you. He only sees the blood of His Son that you will be hidden in.

Chapter 3:

On Your Mark, Get Set, Go!

We have been told to live with hope, faith, and love, but the most important is love (see 1 Corinthians 13). We should love God with all our hearts, souls, and bodies, and love others as God loves us. This means we should not worship any other idols or give power to any addictions. We also should not add to or remove anything from the Gospel, which God has already given us. Then, we should show others the way and tell them that God loves them. God died for us. Are we prepared to die for our fellow man?

The difference between victory and defeat is a matter of corrective thinking in faith. Faith can be understood in different ways. What is your faith? This is what you believe in. You can have faith that you'll get the job that's advertised, but there is a fine line between this faith and hope. Hope is the trust you receive in your thoughts before it drops down into your heart and becomes faith.

Do you know what violent faith is? This is acting on faith that doesn't make common sense. To do this, you have to act out of the norm or go out on a limb. Faith does not operate in the realm of the possible. There is no glory for God in that which is humanly possible. Faith begins where man's power and efforts end. When a man can no longer find possibilities or a way to resolve a situation, God steps in.

God can overcome anything and bring the supernatural into the situation for us. This is why God always chooses people who the world believes won't amount to much. He will use a person who has struggled with the English language to write books for Him. He will operate through them to perform His work. His glory will shine through the situation, and you will know He is busy.

Moses couldn't speak to large crowds because of his speech impairment, so Aaron spoke for him so the crowds could understand what was being said. God chose Moses as a leader and spokesman for His people, the Israelites. He chose fishermen, shepherds, and tax collectors, who at the time, were classified as the simple and lowest-ranking individuals. They could not set out in their own ability to do what they were told if God was not present within them.

Hebrews 11:1–3 says, "Now faith is the substance (the title deed) of things hoped for (a declaration of the action of faith), the evidence of things not seen. (Faith is not based upon the senses, which yield uncertainty, but rather on the Word of God.) For by it (by faith, and as we shall see, it is faith in the cross), the elders obtained a good report (the approval of the Lord)."

Through faith, we understand that the worlds were framed by the Word of God. This refers to Creation and everything that goes with it. So, things that are seen were not made of things that appear. God began with nothing; therefore, a supernatural intervention was needed to create the Universe.

1 Corinthians 2:5 says, "That your faith should not stand in the wisdom of men (speak of any proposed way other than the cross) but in the Power of God (made possible

only by the cross)." 2 Corinthians 5:7 says, "For we walk by faith (Life is a journey, and the Christian will travel to another place), not by sight." This refers to the things we cannot presently see. This is when faith controls us.

The Holy Spirit works exclusively within the parameters of the Sacrifice of Christ. Consequently, He demands that we place our faith exclusively in the cross of Christ. This can only be achieved by coming out of our comfort zones and reaching the extraordinary. We often come up against situations in our life where simply maintaining is not enough. These situations aren't planned, and we have no control over them. There are times that God tells you to do things you would not normally do, and these things will make no sense in the natural world. I'm born from a realm without time and live in a realm with time. You should work to not be subdued by time, but to be a master all the time. Don't look at this as failure; it is meant to draw you back in time so the devil can negate your faith. Faith is a spirit.

Acting on faith often does not rely on common sense at all. In your spirit, you go against all that you can call normal. When following God's ways, we need to swim against the tide, as the salmon do. These fish give all they have, with sheer determination and raw aggression in their persevering attitudes. Those who complete the journey are the ones who set out to complete their Creator's will for this world. They live out their perceived plan—God's intention for their reproduction—and another generation of salmon is born. This is how we ought to run our race: completely dedicated to our end game with our eyes on the end prize, which is our Creator, Jesus Christ

Remember when Peter walked on water and lost faith in himself and God's ability? At that moment, he feared the unknown and began to sink. Then he shouted to Jesus to pull him up out of the water. There is another story of Jesus, who lay asleep on a boat. The disciples woke Him up because they became fearful of the approaching storm.

Jesus then said, "Oh ye of little faith." If the disciples had tapped into their raw faith, they would not have had to wake Jesus; they would've been able to deal directly with the problem. Then there was Lazarus, who was raised from the dead after three days. He was already decayed and stunk terribly, yet Jesus, in his own time, raised him. I believe this was to foreshadow His own resurrection from death that was to come.

So, you see, it's not enough to simply have faith. You have to be able to go that extra mile and prove you have the faith to stand firm in your belief. Faith has worked. It has feet, yet it's nonexistent. It's not just about believing in Jesus, following a religious experience, and having your name written in the church books. Demons believe in Jesus too; they know He exists, and this has been shown in the Bible on many different occasions. They acknowledge His presence and ask His permission, say for instance when they asked if they may depart by moving into the pigs. Demons tremble for fear of God. They know all about Him because they are fallen angels.

Our God is supreme, and He doesn't need to ask permission, but He will never force himself upon a person. He has to be invited in. The Holy Spirit is gentle. He is one of the three who make up God. Believing is fruitless without doing what God wants us to do. Faith that does not result in good deeds is not actual faith.

Faith is the absolute confidence that what you want and what you desire as a child of God is already yours, and it is going to happen. It's knowing what the word of God says and believing in its completeness. You won't need to contemplate or hesitate in your approach. Faith is believing, despite the situations or circumstances that surround you. It is believing with every fragment of your being and standing by it completely.

Regardless of what a situation may look like, you must have complete confidence that what you are hoping for will happen in your life. Without this faith, you can't please God. You have to fight the good fight of faith. If you are going to have returned what Satan has stolen from you, you need to fight in faith.

Satan is the accuser of the brethren; he will send many untrue statements through your mind, like:

- You are not worthy.
- Your sins are too many and too large to be forgiven by Jesus.
- Your children are going to be lost, and they are not safe.
- God doesn't hear you when you call to Him.
- You won't earn enough; you are useless.
- No one actually loves you, and you are all alone.
- **You are sick, and you are going to die.**

You have to remember that Satan is a liar, the father of all lies. When you lie or exaggerate, it may be helpful to remember this statement. Another one of Satan's lies is that all religions, including Christianity, worship the same

God, that all beliefs are equal and are to be respected and accepted.

This is definitely not true. The Lord Jesus Christ must not be confused with the universal god the world worships. That is why we need to fight back in our faith and strike back with everything we have in us. Hell is real. Don't be lukewarm in your faith in Christ. Satan doesn't play the devil.

When You Face Adversity, Use Violent Faith

These situations speak of great faith, and I would like to elaborate on them. A Roman captain (gentile centurion), who was the leader of a hundred men, asked Jesus to heal his sick servant. Then, a Canaanite woman came to Jesus, begging Him to help her with her daughter, who was tormented by a demon.

Matthew 8:5–13 says, "And when Jesus was entered into Capernaum (His headquarters), there came unto Him a centurion, beseeching Him (begging or strongly requesting Him), And saying, Lord, my servant lies at home sick of the palsy, grievously tormented. (This disease was a form of paralysis, which affected the joints and caused spasms, creating intensive pain and suffering. It eventually led to death.) And Jesus said unto him, I will come and heal him (The emphasis is not on the coming, but on who is coming: Jesus Christ the divine healer). The centurion answered and said, Lord, I am not worthy that You come under my roof (referring to being a gentile and showing his own humility) but speak the word only, and my servant shall be healed.

"For I am a man under authority, having soldiers under me: and I say to this man, Go, and he goes; and to another, Come, and he comes; and to my servant, do this, and he does it. When Jesus heard it, He marveled, and said to them that followed, Verily I say unto you, I have not found so great faith, no, not in Israel.

"And I say unto you, that many shall come from the east and west, and shall sit down with Abraham, and Isaac, and Jacob, in the Kingdom of Heaven. But the children of the Kingdom (Israel) shall be cast out into outer darkness: there shall be weeping and gnashing of teeth (This is terribly sad; these people will die a spiritual death without God, thereby going to hell because they rejected Christ). And Jesus said unto the centurion, go your way; and as you have believed (Do you see? It is belief and not doing), so be it done unto you. And his servant was healed in the same hour."

This centurion understood that God had authority over illness without anyone telling him so. He also understood that Christ did not work alone, but as part of the Trinity with understanding beyond His time. He wasn't considered part of the covenant with Abraham. Christ altered His original plan to incorporate the gentile because of the centurion's raw faith.

The way in which the centurion acknowledged Jesus as Lord touched Jesus and showed Him that he was humble and open to God's love and authority. He became His servant and received instruction from Jesus. God's love has no limits, His grace has no measure, and His power has no boundaries.

Jesus was so appreciative of the centurion's attitude that he opened up a pathway to Heaven for all of the gentiles. Here, His own blood that would be spent on the cross would lay the path for the centurion's sins.

Matthew 15:21–28 then says, "Then Jesus went thence (left Capernaum) and departed into the coasts (borders) of Tyre and Sidon. And, behold, a woman of Canaan (a gentile) came out of the same coasts, and cried unto Him, saying, Have mercy on me, O Lord, Thou Son of David; my daughter is grievously vexed with a devil (demon). But He answered her not a word. And His Disciples came and besought Him, saying, Send her away; for she crieth after us. But He answered and said, I am not sent but unto the lost sheep of the house of Israel.

"Then came she and worshipped Him, saying, Lord, help me. But He answered and said, It is not meet (appropriate) to take the children's bread (that which belongs to the Jews), and to cast it to dogs. (Gentiles were looked at as dogs, so in effect, He was testing her faith and humility). And she said, Truth, Lord: yet the dogs eat of the crumbs which fall from their masters' table (The gentile woman accepts the place of the dogs and admits she has no claim to His Grace and throws herself on His Grace as Lord and Savior.). Then Jesus answered and said unto her, O woman, great is your faith: be it unto you even as you will. And her daughter was made whole from that very hour."

The Lord always responds to faith, and only two people are spoken of as having "great Faith." The first was the gentile centurion from Matthew 8:5–13, and the other was this gentile woman.

In the first gentile's advent, Christ tended to the Jews, but they kept rejecting His approach and statute. Because this woman was so desperate, she approached Jesus, calling Him "the Son of David," which only the Jews were privileged or permitted to. This can be seen in two different ways. The first being under deception and hoping she would be mistaken as a Jew, and the second being that she believed things to be and spoke them into existence. As a Jew, she would have approached Christ. A change occurred in verse 25, when she began to worship Jesus and call Him Lord. I could never understand why Jesus tested her so often yet was so kind to the centurion, but then it came to me.

In Luke 11:24–26, Jesus says that if you remove the demon from a person and don't fill that space with the Holy Spirit, then seven more demons, even more wicked, will enter, and this woman will be in a far worse state than before. So, He had to test the mother to see how serious she was in following Him and if she was willing to leave her heathen practices. Then, she would submit her authority under Christ and receive Him to be Lord and Savior of her life. If she passed His test, she would be able to help her daughter and seal herself with the Holy Spirit. This would safeguard them all.

King David was, of course, the earthly lineage of Christ. Christ didn't need anything from man, as He is God and will never cheat. That is why He came through the door (virgin womb) into this world. Satan, however, is not truthful and cheats all the time so he came through a window (as a snake in the garden of Eden).

Jesus further tests the gentile woman's faith, and maybe it was for her to resist the religious spirit's attitude. The religious spirit is the spirit that carries many corrections with it. This is a man-made, diluted Christian version, or a heathen practice. It carries many byproducts of sin, two of them being offense and pride. These two sins may be what was being tested and irritated into a response to act and betray the person's intent.

Through these passages, the gentile woman was clearly tested in both sins, and she was able to overcome. This woman understood fundamental faith and the character of Christ. In her approach and perseverance in faith, she made it possible for her daughter's deliverance. This is now bridged by Jesus' blood on the cross, no longer only for the Jewish nation, but for her whole family and all the gentiles as well.

Jesus showed her that the bread of healing is for the children of God (the Jewish nation), but due to her persistence for the crumbs of bread only, Jesus remarked in verse 28, "This woman would be satisfied with the crumbs of the Living Bread," which are symbolic of Jesus Himself.

Her daughter was made whole from that very moment. His flesh, our daily bread, symbolically brings life to us, just as the manna did for the Israelites.

Charles and John Wesley were two brothers who were given a revelation from God. God showed them that not only can men be justified and liberated through faith, but that it's possible to have a personal relationship with God. This revelation introduced a personal element into our faith.

The movement clarified Jesus' message that salvation was personal and so was the gift of repentance. Romans 10:17

says, "So then faith comes by hearing, and hearing by the Word of God." This refers to actually hearing with your ears and believing with your heart. This is very important in scripture, as this is inscribed onto the flesh tablets of our heart. Then, revelation takes place. Proverbs 22:17 says, "Bow down your ear, and hear the words of the wise, and apply your heart unto my knowledge." Faith comes by hearing, not seeing.

Ephesians 2:8–9 says, "For by Grace (the Goodness of God) are you saved through faith (faith in Christ, with the cross ever as its objective); and that not of yourselves (None of this is of us, but all is of Him): it is the gift of God (Anywhere the word *gift* is used, God is speaking of His Son and His substitutionary work on the cross, which makes it all possible): not of works (Man cannot merit salvation on what he does), lest any man should boast (boast in his own ability and strength; we are allowed to boast only in the cross)." We should accept that everything we receive that is good was from God. Our ability and skills are acquired solely from God.

- Faith plays a crucial role in our salvation.

- Salvation is a step of faith, not by trusting in our feelings.

- Salvation comes by faith in the Finished Work of Christ, not our own efforts, as these count for nothing in the spiritual.

- By faith, we receive the legal right to become children of God (see John 1:12–13).

- By faith, we are moved into action (see James 2:17–20).

- By faith, we experience life change from the inside out.

- By faith, we discover our new identity in Christ (see 2 Corinthians).

Many miracles took place in biblical times, but even more have taken place in the world today. There are thousands of miracles that are written down and even more that have not been journaled. God wants to heal you. He wants to take on the unthinkable and undeniable and even the unbelievable if you dare to believe with a violent faith.

When you are faced with giants in your life, turn your attention to Jesus, then remember those who went before you, like Caleb and Joshua. They saw an opportunity, as they knew who God was and that His promises were real, and they stood steadfast in God's ability and not their own. The other eight spies only saw problems that had to be overcome and did not believe our God could bring all of them to pass.

In Matthew 10:8, it says, "Heal the sick, cleanse the lepers, raise the dead, cast out devils (demons): freely you have received, freely give." Many will argue that Jesus said this to his Disciples and not to all mankind. We are His disciples today, as is outlined in Matthew 9:37: "Then said He unto His disciples, The harvest (souls to be saved) truly is plenteous, but the laborers are few." This means there are not many who are prepared to help the lost find their way back to Jesus. We are responsible for those lost souls, and we all need to spread the Good News to all of mankind.

In Christian living, we follow Colossians 3:17, which says, "And whatsoever you do in word or deed, do all in the name of the Lord Jesus, giving thanks to God and the Father by Him," and 1 Corinthians 10:31, which says, "Whether therefore you eat, or drink, or whatsoever you do, do all to the Glory of God."

We need to grow within and cultivate the virtues of a new life in Christ. But there is something more. We want our new life to be seen as a miracle, and we want to live positively and be admired for having Christ in our lives. Then, others will want what we have, which is Jesus Christ. This is how we should present Jesus Christ to the world. The word *Christian* means "Little Christ." Man sees your actions, but God sees your motives.

The life of Christ didn't end when the Gospel was completed. Christ is alive, and He lives within us if we allow Him and are true to His ways. His life is shown through our lives as living letters to the world. He constantly works with and through them to help others while bringing His will into being. When we are believers, others should be able to observe the fruit of the Holy Spirit manifesting in our lives. The Fruit of the Spirit is love, joy, peace, kindness, goodness, faithfulness, gentleness, and self-control.

You have to allow change to happen, take on Christ's characteristics, and relinquish your old ways. There is no getting away from it; you will not grow or gain anything if you carry on with the same mannerisms as before. Change brings new life, allowing your dead branches (spiritual dead parts) to be removed for good. This will allow for new, rapid, healthy growth to take place in your life.

We need to do all things in the glory of Christ Jesus. This means when working, you think of Christ as your boss. Do everything as though Christ is watching you because He is, constantly. This is in the book of Ezekiel.

Paul states in Philippians 3:17, "Brethren, be followers together of me (be "fellow imitators"), and mark them which walk so as you have us for an example (observe intently)." In this verse, Paul is saying to imitate his actions and live completely for God. We no longer belong to the world, but we come from another kingdom and are only in this world for a short time. In fact, we are passing through and will join all the saints and God when our time on Earth is done. Our God is a saving and loving God, and He has saved us so we might live Godly lives and influence others in a like-minded fashion. Try to be an example of His good deeds with pure intentions and an undiluted doctrine.

Be dignified in speech, then be beyond reproach so the opponent may be put to shame and have nothing bad to say about anyone. The exhortation here is to have self-control, take care of your body like it is a temple, and keep it healthy and well-groomed. It means to have a filter on your tongue that doesn't allow you to say unnecessary nonsense or speak too much.

This means not allowing yourself to say sarcastic remarks or gossip about others. Take control and say that it is not good for you. Even if you want to do it, you should not allow yourself to go there. Having God's long-range purpose for your life and refraining from instant bad needs or behavioral outbursts is a healthy place to be in.

In 1 Timothy 4:13–16, it warns that we shouldn't neglect our spiritual gifts. A new dimension can be achieved through the gift of the Holy Spirit, and this can help us bear fruit in our lives. We should treat each other well and never have anything bad to say, especially in regards to Christ anointed.

Be an example of good and healthy things. Simply living your life as an example for others is better than laying out long speeches and lecturing people on how to act. The effect of living a Christian life should have value. Our effects should make us into powerful men and women for our Lord. We need to stand for Christ Jesus and silence the critics. In these last days, God is calling for His children to move on His behalf, do the things He has called us to do, and do it with our whole heart unto the glory of God.

We were created by Him for a purpose. God has an assignment for each one of us while we are on Earth. It is up to us to seek God and find out what He would have us do for His kingdom during our time here on Earth. God has a plan for each and every one of His children, and it is a good plan. Do it, whatever it is, with your whole heart, mind, body, and strength to the glory of God.

"For I know the thoughts that I think toward you, says the Lord, thoughts of peace, and not of evil, to give you an expected end" (Jeremiah 29:11). We, as believers in Jesus Christ, must walk by faith and not by sight as 2 Corinthians 5:7 says. No matter what it looks like in the natural world, we can rest assured that God is faithful and just in bringing forth all His promises and rewarding those who diligently seek Him.

We are already on the winning side with Jesus Christ, our Lord and Savior. We cannot lose with Jesus. He already paved the way and went before us; He has made the crooked places straight. In Isaiah 45:2, Jesus says, "I will go before you, and make the crooked places straight: I will break in pieces the gates of brass, and cut in sunder the bars of iron." God will not fail us—no He won't, not any of His children—because He loves us so much.

In time, we will all hear that still small voice if we haven't heard it already, the voice of God that leads and guides us, directs our paths, and keeps us from all hurt, harm, and danger. That voice comes through as a change in plans at the last minute, a feeling to go left when you went right, or a feeling that we should call an old friend or family member we haven't spoken to in a while.

God speaks to us in many ways; it is up to us to listen and hear His voice clearly. The Lord is always speaking to His children, but sometimes we are not able to hear Him. There is too much noise in our lives, and these distractions keep us from reaching our full potential and being everything God has called us to be.

You see, the enemy is clever. Satan knows that if he can distract us and pull us away from focusing on God, this will take us away from what God has called us to do. Then, Satan will be able to gain access to our minds. Once he has a foothold in our mind, he can then speak lies to us and pull us even further away from God's plan and purpose. When Satan controls a person's thinking, they no longer have to worry about their actions. This is why we must stay focused on God at all times.

I know from my own personal experience that prayer is the key to having a close personal relationship with the Lord. By seeking Jesus daily in prayer, we draw closer to Him and are able to hear His voice far more clearly. In these last days, we must press in, hold tight to Jesus, and not let go. "I press toward the mark for the prize of the high calling of God in Christ Jesus" (Philippians 3:14).

We need to move beyond the limits we have placed upon our lives and move into a revelation through Jesus Christ. Then, by faith, we can take even more steps to conquer our inner self, with the Holy Spirit leading the way. Take the focus off the world and all its problems and place them on God. No matter how difficult life may get, hold onto Jesus and push forward.

What is within Jesus is far greater than what lies within this world. Jesus the Messiah, Your beauty, glory, and holiness, You are God from God and Light from Light, You are the Great I Am, and all the books in the world could not properly describe the depth of Your Greatness. We know the victory will be ours because of what He has done for us. God will sustain us through His blood and protect us in His love. Despite whatever we may go through, if we hold tight, He will deliver us victoriously to the other side.

Chapter 4:

Believe It and Receive It

When the fallen angels were cast out of the kingdom of God, love left them. This is because God is love. "Love is patient, love is kind. It does not envy, it does not boast, it is not proud. It does not dishonor others, it is not self-seeking, it is not easily angered, it keeps no record of wrongs. Love does not delight in evil, but rejoices with the truth. It always protects, always trusts, always hopes, always perseveres. Love never fails, but where there are prophecies, they will cease; where there is knowledge, it will pass away, everything else will depart but love remains" (1 Corinthians 13:4–7). In life, everything and everyone can leave you, but God will not leave you. This is why Love remains.

1 John 3:1–2 says, "Behold, what manner of love the Father has bestowed upon us (presents that are foreign to this present world and, in fact, come from another world), that we should be called the sons of God (We are "sons of God" by virtue of adoption into the Family of God, derived through the Born-Again experience): therefore the world knows us not because it knew Him not.

"Beloved, now are we the sons of God (We are just as much as a "son of God" now as we will be after the Resurrection), and it does not yet appear what we shall be (Our present state as a son of God is not what we should be in the coming Resurrection): but we know that when

He shall appear (the rapture) we shall be like Him (glorified); for we shall seek Him as He is (Physical eyes in a mortal body could not look upon that body or that Glory, only eyes in Glorified Bodies.)."

God is love. 1 John 4:8 says, "He who loves not knows not God; for God is love." He poured out His love into our hearts through the Holy Spirit (see Romans 5:5). Love is not something God puts into the hearts of the citizens of His Kingdom. Love is something that comes to live in the hearts of His children: the Spirit of King Jesus! The Spirit is love because God is love. There is certainly nothing that can ever separate us from the Love of God. Our spirit and the Spirit of God who lives in us is one. We, Jesus, and the Father all have the same Spirit, so we are one when we give our lives to God (see John 17:20–23).

God loves you; He separated your sins from you, and He loves you. He would never have sent His Son Jesus if He didn't. God has good thoughts toward you, thoughts of peace and not evil. He wants to give you a future with a career. He is concerned for our needs and wants the best for us. Jeremiah 31:3 says, "The Lord has appeared old unto me, saying, Yes I have loved you with an everlasting love: therefore, with lovingkindness have I drawn you."

He knew you before the Earth was even created, and He loved you then, and He loves you now. Ephesians 1:4–5 says, "According to as He has chosen us in Him before the foundation of the world, that we should be Holy and without blame before Him in Love. Having predestined us unto the adoption of children by Jesus Christ to Himself, according to the good pleasure of His Will." He draws you to Him once again. Jeremiah 33:3 says, "Call unto Me, and I will answer you, and show you great and mighty things, which you know not."

People don't understand the depth of God's love. Christ's love must be placed in your heart for you to actually love others, as God will then show you what the true meaning of love is. God gives gifts of healing, miracles, and tongues when we believe in His signs and gifts. These signs and gifts were imparted to prove that Jesus is the Messiah and that the apostles were divinely appointed. There are many gifts God bestows to His children in the form of knowledge or wisdom, like He did with King Solomon.

Today, we are to believe and walk by faith. If it's God's will for us to have a certain gift, we will receive it. If not, we will not. We must love the Giver and not the gift. Learn to become content in every situation you face, whether you are earning well or not. God will supply all your riches in glory because of what Christ Jesus did for you. The promises that the Bible holds are plentiful to those who believe in them. The Israelites refused to believe that God could remodel us into His image, that He could remove the baggage, bad habits, and impure thoughts. But He can renew us from within into a completely different person.

Love was the sacrifice He made in giving His Son, Jesus, who is a divine human being. In John 1:1, the Father sacrificed His heavenly power and glory to become a human being and subject Himself to excruciating suffering and painful humiliation. Jesus explained the fruit of His love when He and His disciples were eating the last supper. Jesus said, "As the Father loves Me, I also have loved you; abide in My love. If you keep My commandments, you will abide in My love, just as I have kept My Father's commandments and abide in His love. This is My commandment, that you love one another as I have loved you. Greater love has no one than to lay down one's life for his friends."

Jesus Christ perfectly showcased all His wonderful traits of the Holy Spirit, not only during His entire ministry but during His arrest, trial, and crucifixion.

Walk in God's Ways

It was the same Holy Spirit that came down at Pentecost with violent winds from Heaven, and those around at the time remarked that it looked like tongues of fire that separated and touched men who spoke in different languages that sounded strange. The scoffers in Acts 2 concluded that all the men who were speaking strangely were actually drunk. God sent His Holy Spirit down in His people.

The people responded by using their gift of a Godly language. This was, in fact, a pouring out of a person's soul before God. Praying in the Spirit is when you use a Godly language to express the inexpressible and praise God through a higher level while your soul empties itself through an edification method.

Hannah sounded as though she prayed in the spirit as well. In 1 Samuel 1:13, Hannah spoke in her heart. Her lips were the only things that moved, yet her voice was silent. In Corinthians, Paul expresses that tongues are proof that God is real to the unbelievers. In 1 Corinthians

14:9–16, Paul explains that speaking in tongues is a heavenly language, that man prays with the Holy Spirit and this language edifies Godly messages to the church.

We need to move forward without reaching back and dragging up the past to rehearse it over again. Forget the past and forgive those who have inflicted problems over you. God can't forgive you if you can't forgive what others have done to you. Speak to yourself and encourage yourself. David encouraged himself when the Amalekites stole their wives, children, and every other belonging they possessed. Paul wants to impart these spiritual gifts to strengthen our walk with God (see Romans 1:11).

1 Corinthians 12:4–11 states that tools are accomplished through the use of Spiritual gifts, and they can be used for the common good of all. Ephesians 3:20–21 says that by the power bestowed within us, we can do infinitely more than ever imagined. Start to speak life over your situation by using relevant scriptures for the area that needs healing or revelation. A change will occur. It may be gradual, so you must continually declare verses over your children and their future rather than criticizing them and verbalizing what they are doing wrong.

There are four creatures in the throne room: the ox, the eagle, the lion, and the human face. These four faces represent the characteristics of God. Never lose heart and never abort the plan God has for your life. The Bible says we need patient endurance to follow the will of God in our lives. These characteristics of the four creatures are what we should imitate in our walk with God. These references are outlined in Ezekiel's vision in Ezekiel 1 and Revelation 4:6–8.

- The oxen symbolize perseverance because they hold onto it in everything they do. They will endure the race till the end. The ox is a hard worker and can carry burdens effortlessly. He works well in a yoke, with others by his side.

- The eagle has insight, foresight, and oversight into situations that are happening and glides the thermals up above the storms. The eagle is proof of the presence of the Holy Spirit. This is a character who takes direction and guidance from the Holy Spirit. He will be patient and wait on the word of the Lord. He pushes the enemy's territory through intercession. He symbolizes an overcomer and will carry the promise of breakthroughs. Eagles are prepared for battle over the enemy. They live in hope, faith, and love. The North American bald eagle has one enemy, and that is the black crow, which lands on his back, sheds his skin away, and kills him if he doesn't act quickly. In a situation with the crow, the eagle will fly as high as he can go, where the oxygen is too low for the crow, and it will fall off the eagle's back. We need to stay close to God so he can help us knock the devil off our back and keep us from moving away from God.

- The Lion speaks of authority and power over a situation. It represents a prince and a powerful person. This power is not as the modern world depicts it, but as God sees it. It symbolizes a leader and warrior for God who stands for the truth. The Lion is brave and places the devil under his foot, where he is supposed to be. He is a strategic bodyguard and gatekeeper. He has victory in Christ. As such, the lion has gone through a period of purification and can expect to walk in victory.

- Lastly, the human factor is to have compassion and deal with the restrictions life imposes on us daily. The man shows contentment in every situation he finds himself in. We should learn these characteristics from the Holy Spirit, which is placed within us.

In John 10:27, Jesus said, "My Sheep hears My Voice, and I know them, and they follow Me." Romans 12:1–2 says, "I beseech you, therefore, Brethren, by the Mercies of God, that you present your bodies a Living Sacrifice, holy, acceptable unto God, which is your reasonable service. And be not conformed to this world: but be transformed by the renewing of your mind, that you may prove what is that good, and acceptable, and Perfect, Will of God."

Many people, unfortunately, are going to hell. Think, for example, that you are in a three-legged pot that is placed on a log fire. At first, the water is cool and pleasant to swim in, but it gradually gets warmer, and soon, it becomes a wonderful jacuzzi. All of a sudden, the wonderful warmth becomes deadly. None of us know when our lives can end; we can, however, make sure we are not in that heating pot.

The three legs that hold this pot up are represented by our attitudes, feelings, and thoughts. These three areas need to be transformed from the world order to a Godly order. Here are a few verses you can read in your own time that can help you make this transformation while spending time with God: 2 Peter 1:10–25, 2 Peter 1:5–7,

Luke 6: 28–42, Proverbs 12:18–28, Hebrew 4:15–16, Romans 5:5, Psalm 42:5–11, John 8:31–32, and Proverbs 18.

You are a spirit, you have a soul, yet you live in a physical body. Your spirit is a lamp of the Lords. God the Father will lead you through the Holy Spirit into all truth. The Holy Spirit gives direction and enlightens your understanding. He leads and teaches through inner prompting, at which point the eyes of your mind will become enlightened. Wisdom then comes from your innermost being. His love is made perfect in you.

Having faith in God will help us move toward our destiny and higher calling in Christ Jesus. God wants to bless His children. In fact, He *loves* to bless us. By having faith in God and believing that Jesus loves us and died for our sins, we know that Jesus will do what He promised to do. All things are possible with Jesus; He can do all things except fail. We have to trust the Lord Jesus Christ and have faith in Him in these last days.

Jesus is a soon-coming King, and with everything going on in the world now, we all need Him like never before. Many people are dying all over the world from COVID-19 and other diseases during this deadly pandemic. Many people are afraid and have lost hope. People who have lost their jobs and don't have enough food to feed their families or money to pay their bills are in desperate need of help.

In 2 Timothy 3:1–4, He said men would be lovers of themselves and pleasures more than lovers of God. Jesus died for the sins of all people, and He loves us all so very much. It's not too late to turn from all sin, repent, and seek Jesus with your whole heart, mind, body, and strength. If you pray to the Lord, confess your sins, and ask Him to forgive you, Jesus will be faithful, and He will forgive you and save you right where you are.

God is able to save every sinner, every person who seeks Him with a pure heart. God desires that our soul prospers and we live in good health (see 3 John 1:2). Just believe it and receive it! God says He will save those who love Him and will protect those who acknowledge Him as Lord. "When they call to Me, I will answer them; when they are in trouble, I will be with them; and honor them. I will reward them with long life; I will save them" (Psalm 91:15–16).

Nothing can happen without God's permission, and God will not allow difficulties unless He has a divine purpose for them. He will then bring this plan to good in your life. If you keep your peace, you will pass the test and God will bring you out better than you were before. God has a perfect plan for us. He never does it all at once, though, just step by step. He wants to teach us to walk by faith and not by sight. All who do not know Christ are veiled. Look into a mirror. The glory of the Lord is changed into the same image from glory to glory (change into Christlikeness). Christ's characteristics will increase and become stronger within you.

As the law of religion in the Old Testament with Moses became dimmer and dimmer, the New Testament took over, and the love of Christ was shone into the world. The Holy Spirit alone can make us into what we ought to be. He will do His work in the parameters of the finished work of Christ's ultimate sacrifice on the cross. It is wonderful, awesome, and merry wise to see Satan lose the battle to us in fear, panic, and shame! Our victory is in Christ Jesus, as is said in 1 Corinthians 15:57.

Aren't you tired of walking on the wrong road? The wrong road takes you to the wrong people, who end up influencing you badly. The wrong road creates the wrong decisions, and it directs you to the wrong results. Every road leads somewhere, so where are you going? I am telling you to take authority and become responsible for your next journey. Ask yourself how tired you are.

What have you become on this road as you've been forced to keep up with everyone around you? What sacrifices have you had to make to win in the world's competitive journey? Are these answers bringing you closer to God? God has a plan for your life, and the enemy has a plan for your life too. Be ready for both. Just be wise enough to know which one to battle and which one to embrace.

Whichever decision you make takes you directly to the same result every time. It's only that the scenery is different, but everything else will be virtually the same. I know because I was there. The right road will lead you to the right situations, the correct people, and the perfect breakthroughs in your marriage or relationships. Traveling on this road in the Lord's ways may not bring you the approval of the world, but it will always have the blessing of God. It will bring you closer to God, and you can receive a counselor to walk alongside you when times get tough. Then you can take on this motto: "When the going gets tough, the tough gets going!"

God can direct you out of situations you feel trapped in. Your faith will increase, and you will move mountains in your life. You'll develop a belief system that will make you want to worship a true and loving God. You need to make the decision today and count the cost. Tell yourself and tell God that you are tired of the same old dusty road you've been walking on. The road toward God may be difficult to walk on at times, and you may experience a few bumps along the way, but you need to stay on it. It may not be a popular route, but the outcome is what's most important. It's a far nicer destination, and it's worth the journey.

I hope that when you hear that knock on your heart, you will answer. Then, you will gain the strength to fight another day as you hurdle all your challenges. You will receive wisdom from above to choose the best course in your journey. The joy of the Lord will give you strength so you can enjoy every single moment, and God's protection and blessings will provide you with a blessed life, and, in turn, you'll be able to bless others.

There was a man named Saul who walked the wrong road for a large portion of his life and made very bad decisions. He killed Christians, Stephen being one of them, who Saul had stoned to death. He killed many others like him and was on his way to kill even more.

Saul was traveling the road to Damascus, as I traveled on the road to Mountain Dale when Jesus intervened. As Saul began to see the town of Damascus, suddenly, an incredible thing happened. The sky around him seemed to light up, and a blinding, dazzling light filled the skies.

It was so brilliantly bright that Saul fell to the ground. He covered his eyes with his arm to try and shield himself from the overpowering strength of its glory. The large party of people around him didn't know what was happening. A loud voice from Heaven clearly spoke to them and said, "Saul, Saul, why are you persecuting me?"

"Who are you?" Saul asked. There was no answer. "Lord?" Saul asked again nervously.

"I am Jesus," came the reply. "I am the one you are persecuting and trying to destroy. Get up and go into Damascus. When you arrive, you will discover what to do."

As Saul eventually got up and opened his eyes, he saw absolutely nothing. He seemed to be completely blind, and all he saw was blackness. His confused and shocked companions lead Saul into the city. He was still blind after three days and refused to eat or drink anything. These three days make me think of Jesus, who was in the grave. This story is symbolic of Jesus saying He went to hell for Saul to become Paul and atone for his sins while He (Jesus) paid the price for his terrible sin.

Jesus sent Saul, who became Paul, to the same people he was to kill. Ananias was called by God to heal Paul's eyes, but he was never the same again. No one ever is the same when they have an interaction with the living God. Paul loved Jesus so much, he was willing to suffer and be constantly persecuted for Jesus Christ. Paul knew that without God, he was nothing, but with God, he was complete. If Jesus could forgive Paul, He would be willing to forgive you too. Today, we are blessed by all of Paul's teachings and have learned so much from him being a part of the Bible as a vessel of God.

Chapter 5:

No More Sitting and Looking

There is no more time for us to sit on the sidelines and wait for God to move on our behalf while we do nothing for God. There is no more time for us to watch others run the race and win while we sit in the grandstand and spectate. Now is the time to get up and do something, take action, and move toward your destiny. Run the race God called you to run and don't look back. Continue to press toward the mark for the prize of the high calling of God in Christ Jesus, just as it's outlined in Philippians 3:14.

We cannot just be hearers of the word of God; we must be doers of the word also. Do something to move God and have faith and belief that He will do something and move on your behalf. "Faith without works is dead" (James 2:26), "for faith is the substance of things hoped for, the evidence of things not seen" (Hebrews 11:1). We must have faith in the Lord Jesus Christ and place all our trust in Him.

Prayer needs action, such as faith (see James 5:15). This faith through Christ Jesus can heal the sick; you need to believe in it. It's no use saying to yourself, "This can never happen, but I'll pray anyway." You will be doing more harm than good because you will be giving fake hope. God looks to your heart, as summarized in Colossians 4:2–4: "pray with a thankful heart and an alert mind for a specific purpose."

Because these are the end times, we look to the powerful people of God who are the forerunners in these strategic times. We are waiting for commands and looking at these men and women to lead us in God's way. We watch how God has used them to lay hands on the sick and even raise people from the dead. They have had thousands standing in front of them as they have preached the infallible word of God as anointed vessels.

For too long now, many Christians who are heavily pregnant with God's word and messages are watching and waiting. They look to others behind the pulpit to do something spiritual. It's time to step out and take your place as you were called to and follow that calling. You can start off as a foot soldier and move on from there. This is the most critical time to live in, but it can be an amazingly exciting and rewarding time as well. We are watching prophecies being fulfilled every day as the coming of our Lord Jesus Christ draws near.

Get ready for God to use you. Step into the correct place and say, "Here I am, Lord. You can use me." Every day, people like you and me are being called to be vessels for God. He wants to use your hands, feet, brain, and whatever else you have to give. Give it to the Lord. There is a move of God, and there is a rumbling in the church to use ordinary people like you.

That anointing you hold is going to break the back of the devil, who is influencing your children, work situation, family, and friends. Some of you have already dreamed and started a ministry but have felt it has failed. Get up and dust yourself off. Get ready to start again. God has power in His word, and He wants to set the prisoners free.

Our Lord wants everyone to pursue Him with all of our hearts and minds, and He wants to birth those dreams, visions, and prayers that He alone has put inside of us. He wants us to try our best to deliver Him to the lost, sick, or weary. We will never have anything born in the natural world until we give birth to the supernatural in our lives.

The same power and spirit that raised our Lord Jesus Christ from the dead are inside you, who have taken Jesus Christ as your Lord and Savior. Many of you doubt or don't realize the power within you. You have a favorite pastor or believe in powerful evangelists but not in your own spirit that lives within you. This gift is in you also; you just may not realize it yet.

Romans 8:11 says, "But if the Spirit (Holy Spirit) of Him (God) who raised up Jesus from the dead dwell in you (and He definitely does), He that raised up Christ from the dead shall also quicken your mortal bodies (give us power in our mortal bodies so we might live a victorious life) by His Spirit that dwells in you (The same spirit is available to us on the premise of the cross and our faith in Christ's sacrifice)."

These days, it can be difficult to trust people, and sometimes, people are not always who they portray themselves to be. We can rest assured that Jesus is our friend, and He is always there, even when others reject us and turn their backs on us. Jesus will never do such a thing. He is so faithful, and He loves us all so very much.

During times of my life when I didn't know where to turn or who to trust, Jesus was my friend, gently calling me to come to Him with that soft still voice. He was always patient with me, waiting for me to turn to Him instead of trusting and depending on man.

He called me out of a sinful life of fornication and saved me from myself. I didn't know how to stop sinning against the Lord on my own; it took Jesus to change me and make me into a better person, a new creation in Christ Jesus. There were times when I wanted to give up and not go on with life. It all seems too surreal and unbelievable that a God can know my every move and love me for who I am, that He has been with me before I can remember.

I thought to myself, *How could God love me? What does Jesus see in me? I am a sinner woman and a fornicator. Why does Jesus love me? How could He?* I realized that the Lord created me, and He knew I would miss the mark and mess up when He was making me. He knew me even before the foundation of the world, before I was conceived in my mother's womb. Jesus knew me, and He loved me then, and He still loves me now.

There is nothing I could do to make Him stop loving me. God is not surprised by my mistakes and shortcomings; He knows me better than I know myself, and He still loves me despite myself. The same way God loves me, He loves you too. It's that unconditional agape love that only God can give to us. When I repented my sins and cried out to Jesus with a pure and sincere heart, the Holy Spirit came into my heart to live and dwell with me.

Be a Vessel for God's Use

I invited Jesus into my life and asked Him to be the Lord over my life. My life has never been the same since that day. Since that day, I have developed a close personal relationship with the Lord Jesus Christ, and I can honestly say that I don't ever regret that decision. If Jesus saved me, surely, He can save you too. I learned to listen to the voice of God and follow his lead. I am still a work in progress, but I am not the woman I used to be, and I owe that to my Lord and Savior Jesus Christ. I chose to allow Jesus to use me and do His will. I chose to be an open vessel for the Lord to fill up and use as He saw fit.

Dr. Griffith Thomas said, "It is not hard to live a Christian life; it is impossible." Through your own effort, you will have far more failure and upset with His spirit and His effort working through you. We are human, and no one has not sinned in life. You will never be perfect when you become a Christian, but you will see your mistakes and want to change them. When you fall, you will want to go back to Jesus and repent.

There will be times you will repent, and after moving forward, you will repeat your sin again. You have to become a new creation in Christ. You will need freeing from your flesh or worldly nature. Jesus will do it when you ask; you only need to take notice of that little, soft voice and obey. Christ can move your struggling to victory, your misery to joy. When the I Am in you leaves, the original I Am (God) moves into you.

Life in Christ is a wonderful thing to have. Paul says the power of the life-giving Spirit—and this power is mine through Christ Jesus—has freed me from the vicious circle of sin and death. In this world, we are subject to laws of every kind. The one universal law is the law of gravity. Jesus was not subject to these laws like the rest of the human population. There was no authority that could bind Him.

When we are Christians, the Spirit of God that is operated by the Holy Spirit lifts us above the world and sin, and sin will no longer have dominion over you or your life. You have been paid for and no longer live under condemnation. If you climb into an airplane and soar into the sky, the plane overcomes the force of gravity. The gravity still remains, but the spirit encapsulates you, and you are free of the repercussions that sin used to have over you. You are now in a covenant that will protect you.

So, step out of a self-life and step into a Spirit-filled life. You must give over and yield yourself to Christ, and He will take over if you allow Him to. Then, you will live a Spirit-filled life that you will never be sorry about. The choice is yours; God does not force man to follow or serve Him. He gives us free will. It is up to us to choose Jesus or not. I chose Jesus. It is my prayer that everyone else will too.

Chapter 6:

Living the Abundant Life

There are many times in our lives when we go through difficult situations, whether it is the loss of a loved one, sickness, persecution, or the loss of money or income. A challenge will come to you, but as you trust in God, it will strengthen your faith. God never said we wouldn't go through hard times, but He did promise He would never leave us or forsake us when we do go through difficulties. We can depend on Jesus. His word is true, and He is not a man, that He should lie (Numbers 23:19), but the living Son of God.

Although we all will go through difficult times on this earth, we can have an abundant life through Christ Jesus. We don't have to be concerned or worried about the cares of this world. There has been a fascination for thousands of years with predicting the end of the world. Many Bible warnings have left us with no doubts that catastrophic events will occur before the coming of Jesus Christ.

When we read the biblical prophecies and that of the apostles, it seems as though we are in the end stages already. Jesus Christ Himself spoke of days that would be so terrible, that days would have to be shortened so people could survive. When reading Revelation, there are a lot of similarities to today's world. Should we take them seriously? I think so. No one will know the day or the hour, but we should always be ready.

In Matthew 11:28, Jesus says, "Come unto Me, all you who labor and are heavy laden, and I will give you rest." In trusting in the Lord and casting all your cares upon Him, God will be faithful and just and will take care of you and work everything together for the good of those who are called according to His purpose (Romans 8:28).

We have to trust God to take care of us and have faith and belief that He will do it. Philippians 4:19 says, "But My God shall supply all your needs according to His riches in Glory by Christ Jesus." God is good, and He desires to have a close personal relationship with all of His children. Through prayer, talking to Jesus daily, and spending time alone with the Lord every day, we can draw closer to Jesus and have fellowship with Him.

How can you stop yourself from worrying? Pray about everything. A prayer prayed in faith can be one of thanksgiving. Paul prayed in Philippians 4 that Christians will have constant joy and not place any cares on themselves. Place your prayers in God's hands and leave them there. A farmer must scatter his seeds after plowing the earth well, then have faith they will grow. This is how you should handle your everyday cares as you cast them onto Jesus.

When you pray like this, God will stand guard over your thoughts and heart. Your thoughts determine your life, so you must train your mind in corrective thought patterns. Take your mind captive under the authority of Jesus Christ (see 2 Corinthians 10:5).

By putting Jesus first in your life, you are making Him the head of your life. Trust in Him alone by depending on Him for all your needs, hopes, and desires. Even during a global pandemic, Jesus is with us, and He cares. Even during this season of COVID-19, you can make it, and you can have an abundant life through Jesus Christ our Lord and Savior. Living for Jesus and being a part of His heavenly kingdom provides an abundant, blessed life. It's better than worldly possessions or insignificant things that will not last on this earth. The abundant life is a life with Jesus now and into eternity. You must trust in the Lord and have faith that He will take care of your every need and desire.

Conclusion

Dear reader,

It is my sincere hope and prayer that this book has touched your heart and has given you revelation, hope, and encouragement to know that Jesus Christ is more than enough. The Lord is bigger than any problem, illness, or circumstance you may be going through. God sincerely cares, and He desires to have a relationship with you and be the Lord over your life. To those of you who have not accepted Jesus as your Lord and personal Savior, I invite you to do so now.

It is my deepest desire that everyone who has not yet accepted Jesus Christ into their heart will seek the Lord now and develop a close personal relationship with Jesus before it's too late. We need to acknowledge that we are all sinners, and no human, except for Jesus, has not sinned (see Romans 3:23 and Luke 18:13). God's word says it's important that we acknowledge this fact and repent our sins daily.

Read this sinner's prayer, believe it in your heart, and become a changed creation in our Lord Jesus Christ. If you want to step into this new life of unconditional love from the one and only Savior of the world, Jesus Christ, it is very easy to do so. First, believe in your heart that Jesus Christ is the Son of God and that He was born of a virgin womb. He lived, died, and rose from the dead, and on the third day, he rose again, just for you! The second step, you must confess to Jesus with your mouth by praying the following prayer:

"Heavenly Father, I acknowledge that I am a lost sinner. Lord Jesus, I believe that you are the Son of God and that you came and died for my sins. Thank you, Jesus, for dying for my sins. Your body was wounded and bruised, and by Your Blood, I have been forgiven, and by Your wounds, You have purchased healing for me. I repent of all my sins and wrongdoings now. I ask You to forgive all these sins that I know of and those I don't, and I ask You to come into my life as You wash me clean.

"I am so sorry for everything I have done that goes against Your will and Your plan for my life. I give You full control of my life, and I ask that You help me walk in Your love and grace. I thank You, Jesus, for loving me unconditionally, and I ask You to please come live inside of me and be Lord over my life and make me a new creature in You. Lord Jesus, I now receive You as my Savior, my Healer, my Lord, and my God. I open the door to my heart and life for You to take control. Take the reins of my life. I want to be led by Your Holy Spirit. Father, I thank Jesus that You are now my Savior, and Lord, that I am now Your Child. Amen"

I am praying for each and every one of you, and I love you all with the love of Christ Jesus. At the end of this section, I have included a list of scriptures that will help you get started on your journey to wholeness and an amazing relationship with our Lord and Savior Jesus Christ.

"I (Jesus) tell you, No: but, except you repent, you shall all likewise perish" (Luke 13:3). Repent your sins and be converted so your sins may be blotted out (see Acts 3:10).

Try to remember the price Jesus paid for the sins you've committed and realize the ugliness of sin and try to resist it in the future.

If you confess your sins, He will forgive you, as He is faithful, and He will no longer remember them. He will clean us in His righteousness (see 1 John 1:9 and Romans 10:10). Isaiah 55:7 says, "Then let the wicked forsake his way, and the unrighteous man his thoughts, and let him return unto the Lord . . . for He will abundantly pardon." Speak from your heart and mean what you say, and the Lord Jesus Christ will forgive all your sins.

Believe statements, such as "For God so loved the world, that He gave His only Begotten Son, that whosoever believeth in Him should not perish, but have Everlasting Life" (John 3:16). Romans 10:9 states that if you confess with your mouth and believe in your heart, submit yourself under the authority of Christ, and accept by faith His promises, now that Jesus Christ is in your heart, you can have the experience of being born again.

Obtain a Bible and find a good Bible-based church that will teach you the word and desires of God. Write down today's date in the front of the Bible. This date is a significant marker in your life. Let this be a confirmation that you have dedicated your heart and life to the Living God. You are a child of God and are now received in love. When resisting the devil, remind him by pointing him to the date you gave your life to Jesus Christ and rebuke him. Begin reading the Bible on your own and ask God to reveal Himself to you through His word. Most importantly, spend time alone with the Lord every day.

The word of God is your weapon against the demonic world. It is known as the two-edged sword and will help you in defending yourself, as Jesus did against Satan. Satan has been defeated and waits for judgment. He still operates through people and will attempt to attack you and lead you into declaring defeat and leaving your winning position. Don't stand for these mind games. Rebuke him and send him on his way. Satan has become your biggest enemy, and he is constantly looking for ways to trap you.

Constantly talk to Jesus. You don't need to be formal or close your eyes, but talk to Him as your best friend, a father, or a brother. He is a constant ally who will be there for you anytime you want to chat, in every situation. Talk to Him throughout your day and create a strong relationship with Him. Remember to praise and worship Him regularly.

The word *baptism* comes from the Greek word *baptizo*, which means "to immerse." You need to be baptized. This is a symbol of your present self dying as you are submerged into the water rather than buried under the soil. This is an act of obedience to God's instructions. Get baptized in Jesus' name for the remission of your sins. In Mark 16:16, Jesus says, "He who believes and is baptized shall be saved."

Have people pray for you to receive the Holy Spirit if you have not received it already, according to Acts 2:38–39. Find a Christian fellowship with born-again-believing Christians. This fellowship should follow the Gospel and should not have a diluted translation. Try to keep the picture of coal on fire in mind. When it is separated from the pile for too long, it grows cold and dies. As Christians, we need to fellowship with other Christians, even though we are in different stages of our walk with Jesus. It is important to remember that we must keep our trust in Jesus and not in man.

To those of you who already have a close personal relationship with Jesus, I pray your relationship stays strong and that your faith never wavers.

May the Lord Jesus Christ bless and protect us all during this pandemic and at all times. I love you all with the love of Jesus Christ. Bless you, and may you be blessed with the riches of His Grace; with the treasures of His Love; with the comfort of His Mercies; with the strength of His presence; and with the touch of His Care.

Below, I have provided 10 scriptures from the King James Bible that can be helpful to you as you travel on your path to God.

- Romans 10:9 – "That if you shalt confess with your mouth the Lord Jesus, and shall believe in your heart that God has raised Him from the dead, you shall be saved."

- Matthew 11:28–30 – "Come unto Me, all you that labor and are heavy laden, and I will give you rest. Take My yoke upon you, and learn of Me; for I am meek and lowly in heart: and you shall find rest unto your souls. For My yoke is easy, and My burden is light."

- Acts 2:38 – "Then Peter said unto them, Repent and be baptized every one of you in the Name of Jesus Christ for the remission of sins, and you shall receive the gift of the Holy Ghost."

- Romans 12:1–2 – "I beseech you, therefore, brethren, by the mercies of God, that ye present your bodies a living sacrifice, holy, acceptable unto God, which is your reasonable service. And be not conformed to this world: but be ye transformed by the renewing of your mind, that ye may prove what is that good, and acceptable, and perfect will of God."

- Romans 13:11 – "And that, knowing the time, that now it is high time to awake out of sleep: for now is our Salvation nearer than when we believed."

- Proverbs 18:21 – "Death and life are in the power of the tongue: and they that love it shall eat the fruit thereof."

- Psalms 30:5 – "For His anger endureth but a moment, in His favor is life; weeping may endure for a night, but joy comes in the morning."

- 1 Corinthians 2:9 – "But as it is written, Eye has not seen, nor ear heard, neither have entered into the heart of man, the things which God has prepared for them that love Him."

- 2 Timothy 2:15 – "Study to show thyself approved unto God, a workman who needs not to be ashamed, rightly dividing the Word of Truth."

- 2 Timothy 2:22 – "Flee also youthful lusts: but follow Righteousness, Faith, Charity, Peace, with them who call on the Lord out of a pure heart."

References

Lessin, R. (2007). *His footsteps, my pathway.* Christian Art Gifts.

Richman-Abdou, K. (2017, October 3). *Kintsugi: The centuries-old art of repairing broken pottery with gold.* My Modern Met. https://mymodernmet.com/kintsugi-kintsukuroi/

Swaggart, J. (2006). *Holy bible containing the old and new testaments authorized king james version: Translated out of the original tongues and with previous translations diligently compared and revised: The expositor's study bible.* Jimmy Swaggart Ministries.

Van Zyl, J. (1996). *Victory over the devil's attacks.* Stanger Christian Centre, Faith in the Word Ministries.

www.ingramcontent.com/pod-product-compliance
Lightning Source LLC
Chambersburg PA
CBHW062150100526
44589CB00014B/1765